AF430238

Madness In Milwaukee

A Poetry Collection

Annette Towler

Yellow Dress of Summer

Waking up at three am to the cat nibbling my toes

Tossing backward and forward,

Falling into the abyss of sleep.

Every childhood sweetheart appears:

We are friends with John Travolta.

Not the Travolta of later years

grieving the death of a wife

The young John of a thousand dancers

Coats so white they shine

The yellow dress of summer

We sparkle and throw our arms aloft

Astaire and Ginger gaze in awe

At John's prowess on the disco floor

John Travolta is my best friend

I dance in my dress of summer

I screech the words of Brothers Gibb

I laugh with John like no other

The yellow dress of summer

Hanging in my wardrobe space

Remembering the good times

High School and Disco grace

Luncheon with you and Manet

My fingers stroke your beard

Your fingers slice through my hair

Cutting the meat into cubes marinating

Luncheon with you; Lunch

Turning into dinner with favorite artists

Manet, Turner, le dejeuner in Paris

Red Wine soaks the meat, firm in the pot of Holland.

Your hands sweep across my body

Admiring, complimenting

You speak of April because it is the wickedest month of all

The artists fly in to guide us, to invite us

We sup with Manet and dream of Rome.

In Rome, we are Greg and Audrey

Flying down the road on a scooter

Built for one

No thought of food

Just us

Starving hungry with nothing to wet our appetite

Only us with Manet

Leonardo catches a ride

If this be madness, good let's have it

The stupidness of first kiss

Emotion mixed with passion

We find Sartre very witty

You tell me my beauty is breathtaking

Your heart is pounding

Monet clutches your chest in a moment of bliss

Beatitudes fly in to speed up the feast with all the

Contemporary painters

The dreamers, love makers

We settle down, your arm wrapped around me

Madness flees the scene

We are alone with Manet

The perfect dream

The Cat for Kids

Stretching out along the sofa,

The cat for Kids

Closes her eyes

To watch me sleep,

Watching over me, just a kid.

The greenest eyes in the Caucasian kingdom,

Mixed with fur and appetite for new possibilities,

After loss,

The cat comforts the kid inside me, still

twisting and sucking her thumb.

The soft touch of paw

On my cheek,

To remind me of the corner store,

All the kids swinging,

Sucking the gobstoppers of youth.

The cat of comfort

Refuses to bury the loss

To avoid the pain of grief, choosing instead to watch

 over me,

a kid zooming down the country road on a kid's tricycle.

The cat of loss

Raised by a stranger

Scooping out the litter, tossed

Onto the pavement

Old into new kid on the block.

Oswald Tree

Gorgeous top of cream

      Delivered each morning to the family along the slice of street

Strip of bacon sizzling in the pan

      Fractured egg splatter in the bowl

Within the hamlet of Oswald Tree

Primary school children sip

      The straw of life

Hopping from pavement to scotch

      House for the public

line the downtown main street

Oswald Tree is calling me

      Fat Black Stout sipping from straw to strainer

Tea in the morning to recover from the

      Leaves of hanging

In the English alley

Oswald Tree

     Noose around Neck

Thin Welsh Country

     Fight to hold claim

Bitter to Lager in the warmth of the drain

Oswald Tree

     Call me close

Sip of brandy in a lullaby

     Spoon for the baby

Crave and Cry

White Boy
Summer

White Boy Summer

Three local boys out for a ride

A warm summer day in Texas

Three boys of Jasper

Having fun

Pound Pound

Rip Rip

Blood boils in southern Texas

Heat is rising

Local boys

Having fun with James

Teasing, Prodding, Poking

Pound Pound

Rip Rip

Summer picnic time

Dirt kicks high along the gravel lane

One mile

Still alive

Rip Rip

Pound Pound

Three Jasper boys

Proud and Loud

All about Madness

Connected through fever

Hospital patients rise out of their beds

Screaming for ventilation

Knitting in a circle

Therapists gander and gaze

Navel twist from the needles

Knotty depression at the poker table

Dice full of emotional baggage

Flung across the table

The croupier yawns

Politicians howl at the moon

Gaza serene and lovely

A blink to watch it disappear

President shrieks and hums a tune

The wretched Ratched draws my attention

Insanity inside the hospital

Walk inside the bank with Murphy and the boys

Write a check so that everything is alright

Madness is everywhere

Truth has taken a jet to an exotic place

Where we whisper in guarded, hushed tones

The king is still as mad as when

he ripped off his old clothes

There is madness in the stones of Milwaukee

I watch the man on the bike

Climb up the hill

Soaring like a whale

Sprockets for spouts

Puffing and steaming in the thick of incoherence

In the sweat and rancor of a thick June day

Madness as the masks are ripped off inside the supermarket

Only those who are fully

needled and clean

Insanity inside the bottle of Orange squash

Those with masks stare in awe

At those who have come to life in the malls

Gaping eyes wide open

Zombies return to clutch perfume

Spray on their hollow wrists

Inside the coffee shop

The barista is hearing voices in the back of the store

Counting the beans again and again

Dark roast, spit out the decaf

One count, trillion count

More beans, don't spill the beans

Efficiency in automation

Along the river, I run and cough a thousand times

One step, two steps

Glad to be alive and thriving

Not just awake, transformed

From caterpillar to butterfly

Madness takes new form.

Icarus Grows Up

I knew him when he was a lad

Flying through the English sky on a Saturday night

Soaring up into the clouds, grey clouds,

Bitter cold in the 70s

Palm trees in the 90s

He grew up and moved to Barcelona

Because the beer is better in old town Spain

As a boy

always in the chemistry lab

Shining his magnet on the fleas, trapped in the window

Everyone laughed, apart from me.

They loved to hear his tales of soaring up into the sky

Brightness at birth, stories so shining

They eclipsed other tales of normalcy

Now he has grown up for the Spanish siesta

A man torn by the wings of desire

Senoritas on all sides

Senors with bull horns

Waiting to pierce his weathered skin

too much sun

On his face, too much money, too much space

Icarus grew up from being a boy

The sun refused to be another of his toys.

The Tidiness of the Landscaped Garden

There are no weeds in the manicured garden

Every cuticle of carefully arranged flowers is placed in a symmetrical line

Brows of Begonias line the windows, shuttered to keep out the mad sun

Each Sunday the man from Mexico City dons his hat at the lady of the house

Noting her taut skin, like a white orchid petal

stripped of moisture

The lady of the upper east side home in Milwaukee looks out behind the blinds

Blinking at the man, brown from the sun

With eyes the color of smoky coffee

The kind of man that she dreams of when her husband, wealthy in his suit

Touches her in an orderly, respectable way

Tidy in his touch without caress.

The visitors to Upper east side gaze at the landscaped garden

Imagining the wealth inside the house

Passersby with mascara for eyes and tattoos for protection

With the lust of a hungry, passionate lover

The lover who can afford a Mexican taco from the truck, on the corner.

The woman of wealth and longing closes her eyes imagining

Standing outside the taco truck from hell, sucking in the juices from the

Guacamole as the gardener tucks a flower into her hair

For the senorita

The woman wonders what it feels like to feel the cold, damp rain on his back

As he trims and snips the carefully arranged shrubs, moist with dew

Coiffured and collected, the woman closes the window

Shuts her eyes, not ready to say adieu.

Milwaukee River on Memorial Day

'Twas brilliant and the slimey toads

Did gamble and giggle in the waves

All mystic were the bottles Oh

And the memes rath for grabbing, not the Trumpian way.

Beware the conspiracy, my solo run!

The graffiti spoke to me

As I ran along the riverbank,

Waiting for the jaws that bite, the claws that catch!

Yet twas bleeding awesome, as Eliza Doolittle might say

The waves splashed with the seagulls soar

There was no jubjub bird, just the sound of roar

I shunned the frumpy evil stare of the Bandersnatch

That took me unaware

I had no vorpal sword in hand

Merely a hand-held drink, so long I sought

I rested by the bridge of butterfly

And stood a while in thought.

And as I stood there with many thoughts

The Jabber of Trump, with orange flames,

Came roaring and whiffling through the riverbed

And burped as it came!

One tweet, One too many too! And through and through

I run like a blade, snicker-snacker!

Goodbye Orange Jabber, and with a lift of head

I went galumphing back home to the cat

The cat of a thousand wisdoms said to me

"And hast thou Jabber treats for me?

I picked the cat up in my arms, my beamish beauty!

O absolutely fabulous day along the Milwaukee river!

Salut, Salut Memorial Day

The cat meowed in her joy.

It was absolutely brilliant and the toads were

Gone and gimbled no more in the waves

All misty were my eyes of blue

And the memes disappeared, tweet so long, adieu.

Thin-brimmed Mister with Miss

Thin-brimmed mister with Miss

Mission into Milwaukee

Mister gives kiss, Miss is in bliss

Mister likes his Miss, she is his.

Milky ice-cream with his kiss

Miss licks lips, it is his wish

Into Third Historic Milwaukee, it is sizzle, nix fix

Into his dive, Mister with Miss

Fix Gin Fizz, sip, sip, zip, zip

Mister spies fixer, winks, sniff, sniff

Mister with Miss

High in bliss

Miss misses it, sniff, sniff, wink, wink

Fix it, Fix it Mister

Miss is giggly, Mister is sick

Mister is insane, Mister in intensive

Miss is in pain, Miss is his.

Kohler Tour

Tuesday afternoon in the Village of Kohler,

The tour guide is full of knowledge and experience

Already in love with the first of the men

Victorian, handsome, Austrian descent

The tour guide's belly full of rump

Full of love for the old-fashioned men

The ones who sweep you in the cradle with their hand

The tour continues through the bathroom and bidets

Of Kohler design, meshed against the wall

Showers, basins, radio blast, soap holder, tear filler

Tour guide relishes the farming tools, basic implements

Intervention to clear the fields, to build the factory.

From overseas they came, escaping the smoke from the Austrian chambers

Sitting snug inside the worker cottage, pints of beer without umbrage

Safe in the terror of industrial furnace, the workers build the factory

The design pieces, from iron to gold, splash from the shower

Manufacturing village, built from the minds of creators and humanitarians.

Breathless Runner

Many are still asleep, as this runner jogs to the Oak Leaf Trail,

Checking the watch, strapped around the thin wrist, bereft of fat and gristle,

Watching the sun rise above the brilliant white art museum, beckoning

with the display of art to visit,

this runner waits.

This runner watches the two African American men glide on their bikes,

smiling at the freedom of the bike path,

peddling with all the breath they can muster as they close their eyes,

imagining a world where everyone is afforded the same.

This runner waits for them to pass, takes a

Deep breath and runs frantically up the hill,

Catching her breath, exhaling the air,

Breath in, breath out

With the lungs rising and falling as she ascends the climb from Veteran's Park

To the tip of the hill, where the lime scooter, abandoned,

Awaits her before she stops to catch a breath,

The air torn and heavy with the humidity of the morning,

This runner waits.

This runner waits for the summer of heat to pass

Friday night shots into Saturday morning, yellow tape

Circulating around the car park, car

Smashed into post,

This runner watches and waits and

Continues into the Cambridge woods,

The lone deer beckons with the look of

Peace and solitude that soothes the memory

Of the car, the shots, the gun that triggers

A memory from the past,

This runner watches, waits,

This runner runs.

The Cat and the Lizard

Inside the building, the cat sits on the perch, overlooking the tree that

contains the bird, the solitary bird, the lonely bird,

crying out to all the other birds for company.

The cat sits alone and closes her eyes, dreaming of a hot sun in the desert

where the lizard basks in the rays, dreaming of a time when

giant lizards roamed the land, searching for company,

isolated from all usual things, searching for the meaning

that lizards seek of why

it is necessary to crawl on all fours when the cat can spring up

into the air inside the condominium without a care and be happy

with just the human, never yearning for the lizard, who

craves belonging in the hot yellow heat.

The lizard continues to yearn for the cat of company, the cat

that roamed with the lizard in a dream composed by the human, who lives

in the condo, mask less, once homeless, connected, protected by the

cat who adores her, will not abhor her, just like the lizard

twisted, conflicted, in the strong sun of the desert, never

groaning, moaning, just shouting for connection, the lizard

lies out in the hot yellow sun, while the cat looks at the bird

closes her eyes, at one with the sun.

A Visit from the Plumber

The leak starts on a Tuesday, rather than a Monday, because

that would be too ironic, to start the drip, drip onto the head on the day

when all the residents in the building groan and grumble about being forced to rise from the bed of comfort and to touch toes on the carpet, faded over all the years, faded

from all the pressure of the toes that have stamped and stomped each and every Monday

This leak starts on a Tuesday.

Like any problem that needs to be solved, the owner of the condominium, points the

finger at herself, wondering if it was the mass of hair that had fallen off the top of head,

No chemo, no wig, just age and decline, the strands of hair that can be grasped by fingers that demand that the hair be snapped and strained, the plumbing problem is the human problem

The leak of all leaks starts on a Tuesday.

One wonders if it is the air conditioner and when that is ruled out, again the finger points to the upstairs bathroom, where the owner sits every morning, contemplating runs and human relationships that can be so complex, as complex as

the plumbing situation.

The kind of problem that is examined every day of the week until the problem is resolved, and Monday starts to seem like Saturday when the weekend stretches out, into one long festival full of plumbers, maintenance men, and neighbors with holes

in the pipes and inside their walls, that threaten to spill out into

other homes, the kind of problem that starts on the weekend

and by Tuesday is near death's end.

The plumber arrives with Sherlock suggestions, the resident dew-eyed in the
Ms. Watson role, the animals vanish into the bathrooms and closets, hearing
the drill that tears the wall down to reveal the plumbing inside the wall,
adjoining the neighbor with one cat alone, the boxes are staggered inside the
neighbor's condominium in case there is a chance that

she will be found alone.

The plumber arrives and the drip appears and disappears much like the
memory of fear throughout the years that scurries and waltzes around the
pipes and the vaults, the fear that tears through the building even though the
masks have gone.

The drip that arrived on the Tuesday is still present with the owner,
contemplating her place in the world, former teacher now therapist, the mind
is under duress, relaxing at the solution that the plumber has brought.

eigh-bor?

Battle with Frank Gallagher

Gallagher! Gallagher! Lurching bright
In the pub crawls of the night,
What immoral hand on thigh
Could thwart thy drunken revelry?

In what distant shots or pints
Burnt the glaze of thine eyes?
Oh how Sheila dare he aspire?
With her hand, dare seize desire?

And what of Monica, oh such art,
Could twist the embers of your heart?
And when her heart begins to beat,
Her dreadful hand and what dread sleep?

What the hangover? What the brain?
What bar stool do you claim?
What the amber? What dread stout
Dare its deadly blackness grasp?

When the Gallaghers threw down their pains,
And water'd garden with their tears,
Did Frank smile his work to see?
Did Frank who drank the ale make thee?

Gallagher! Gallagher! Lurching bright
In the pub crawls of the night,
What immoral hand on thigh
Could thwart thy drunken revelry?

The roots of toes and feet

Along the single track, the tree no longer in existence

catches my attention with roots of strength and depth

curling up towards the sky like a tower cut from the limbs

yet with the roots still alive, needing to rise towards the sky,

invisible to the millions of native trees who breath, despite the lack of air.

Along the single track, my feet tread along the stones, the roots of past

runners, no longer present, their roots still present in the steps that

we run, over hills and through the cluttered and jumbled mixture of our

minds, until there is an awakening of thoughts, a new observation that the

thoughts

in our heads are merely ideas, suggestions, tricks on the brain, and within our

bodies

is the beat of a baby, small and vulnerable.

The towers of Conrad's madness rise around me as I continue to run along the

path of nature, my eyes glazing over, wondering when they will fall, wondering

If I will fall, carefully navigating the roots embedded in the ground, roots of sturdiness, conscientiousness, my roots gained from lessons, development of

self, contemplating the folly of a man, a man who wanted everything and

Lost it in his ivory tower of knowledge because knowledge is important and it changes, like the tree, roots firm in the logic, the importance of refining the propositions, the hypotheses, the branches, just like my legs every changing with age,

age that brings the realization that emotions are real.

The emotions that I bring back to the building after my run, still changing and evolving

not escaping my notice, calming and controlling, like the branches on my legs, the spider veins winding their way up my legs, still study and ageing, my mind relaxes with thoughts of the tree stump, not dead but quiet after many years of existence, like my legs still alive after many miles of friction, legs resting on the sofa after a long week of runs, gazing at Magritte's painting that depicts the folly of Almayer, realizing that Magritte shines a light on our impulses, all of us wanting and needing to live forever, for our legs to keep going and for the tree trunk to be ever alive.

Tacos with Tolle

The meeting with Tolle is located in the west suburbs of Milwaukee, not the

Tolle of fame and fortune, whose quotes are smeared like guacamole all over the

Internet wall.

This is the Tolle whom classmates described as a little odd, a little

peculiar, whose knowledge of the book of Revelations made them wonder

if he had gone a little stir-crazy when he watched the school bullies

being tossed into the toxic taco hell.

A rose waits for me on Tolle's reserved table beneath the eye of the well-endowed

barmaid, who describes the fish-filled tacos that are the most popular menu
on the item, the kind of fish that Tolle hopes will get him a place through the
heavenly gates, as those

who live in the city toss their sombreros into the fiery furnace, mixed with

bacon bits and iceberg lettuce.

This is the Tolle who wept by the stream when his conventional wife passed
away, the kind of wife that many gentlemen would be proud to say

This is my lady.

And now the Tolle with the broken heart looks at me, hoping that

I will run away with him to a land fueled by solar power and self-sufficiency, away

from all the men who want me to nibble quesadillas with chips and salsa hell on the side.

In another time, another place, I would have run with him into the Upper Peninsula, loving the all-American boy who reads from the bible, not every day, just

On a Sunday.

4th Of July

Dazzled. I trip and listen to your softly spoken words.

Giddy like a child, swinging too high in the state-run park,

Catching your words and the scent of you, the life in you.

Dazed. Confused at the toddler inside of me.

Listening to your words, dashing down the cobbled street,

On the non-electrical scooter, the pushing kind,

Not the pushy type, that is you.

Demented. Not when with you, my hand snug inside

your hand. How is it that one good soul can change another one?

In a spectacular and normal moment, the normalcy of being

with you, just you.

Dawn. The moment when you sneak behind me to make me giggle

at the stuffed animals inside the nature museum because you know they

remind me of the horror films, of Norman Bates, they remind me of

my mother. With you, the horror film goes away.

Dreaming. The moment when my eyes close and the schoolyard appears in

bright and bold colors of marbles, hopscotch, and chalk that kids used

on the playground to mark their territory. With you, there is no mention of
property.

PARK
CLOSED

Blue Bird of Mexico

Inside the apartment, inside my beating heart

Incased inside the asymmetrical walls are memories,

symbolized by knick-knacks, souvenirs from holidays.

Occasionally, my eyes fall on the blue bird of Mexico and

it normally occurs when I am playing Calexico, whom not a lot of people know.

Inside these wobbly arteries of the condominium, erected during a time when

it was not polite for a girl to yell, my heart beats even faster at the fantasies and

dreams that seem more real than real.

The blue bird of Mexico constructed with porcelain, the finest in the country of

waterfalls, ancient places, people with hearts, big and bursting

watermelons. Alone with the blue bird, I think of the day that my mother

died.

There is a part of me that wants to fly away with the Blue Bird of Mexico, catching

the cat in my hands, the three of us sailing over the Atlantic and landing back in the street complete with chippie, church, and corner store full of chocolate.

For a moment I am in flight until landing back in the condominium, I spy

the Blue Bird from Mexico frozen in time on the coffee table, no longer

mobile, a memento from a holiday of the past.

The Women of Milwaukee

Some are tall, some are short, some are carrying those few extra pounds to show their

curvaceousness, some are

Alone.

The women of Milwaukee, such variance in their who, what, how and

Why and, at night, some look at the sky waiting for the suns and moons to collide

And to bring Galahad or the hero of Poldark into their lives who doesn't care

About the extra tires.

Some are sweet, some are cynical, some are torn, some are whole, the women of

Milwaukee, greeting, welcoming, collective groaning, the padding

to protect the fractured heart.

The Women of Milwaukee, resplendently wrapped in mid-west charm, beads of

love curl around their wrists, some scatter petals onto the lawn, some scatter

confectionary wrappers onto the rug, next to the hearth, next to the empty

throne.

Some are sacred, some are scared, some are sacrificial, some are aware that the voices

from childhood never quite go away, so the Women of Milwaukee build a fence around

their hearts, to escape Cupid's arrow, to save them from the dogs that bark.

The Women of Milwaukee enjoy the fine mid-west life full of beer and brats, cheese and

chatter, volunteering until the empty clatter stuns them into silence or puffs them into

dragons, some hissing, some kissing, some tiring of too much listening and

The Women of Milwaukee carry on living.

Taboo Tattoo

Oh no!
Taboo Tattoo
Onto rue.

Tattoo for you
Tattoo for two
Hot boy you
Tot or two

Taboo no fool
Oh you cool
No you rule
Blow snow too

Cot for two
On your stool
You do dope
You no fool

You Taboo
Oh you drool
Told you fool
Dope got you

Freud, no longer in fashion

I recall the time when he was all the rage, everything was simmering beneath

the iceberg, not the lettuce.

The ID was in, and members of polite society did not care for the rigid tones of
the super, overloud ego.

Today, Freud is forgot, like a rejected lover, swipe left, nobody likes Freud,

No longer in fashion.

In his time, he was the Kardashian King, hypnosis, free association with a cup
of gin, yet now, he is last year's model.

Freud no longer on the model floor, his therapeutic methods trounced, his
erotica scorned, poor Sigmund, feeling like a nerd on the somatic experience
floor.

There was a time when he ruled the land, stretched out fully on the recliner
lounge, his analysis sizzled like a sirloin steak, young women fainted with
every look that he gave, too bad he is out of fashion.

Freud, once an ally in the therapist camp, to most he is jaded, like an ex-lover

Bounced.

Sigmund, I sometimes think of you when I'm sitting alone in my therapist
stew and I dream of a day when you rise again, so that every therapist writes
reaction formation with a swift Sigmund pen.

Until the day that you come back, just know that this therapist cuts you some
slack.

Eli
Says "Hi"

www.ingramcontent.com/pod-product-compliance
Lightning Source LLC
Chambersburg PA
CBHW060218120726

48004CB00008B/1863